© Copyright 2018 Rose Publishing

All rights reserved. No portion of this book may be reproduced, stored in a retrieval system, or transmitted in any form or by any means - electronic, mechanical, photocopy, recording, or other - except for brief quotations in printed reviews, without the prior permission of the publisher.

ISBN 978-0999116708

The ABC's
of Christian Living

WRITTEN BY LAURIE GWALTNEY

ILLUSTRATED BY LAURIE GWALTNEY
AND REV. FRANK MACHINA

A special thanks to my dad who inspired me,
my family who supported me,
and my God who never gave up on me.

***All have sinned and fall short of the glory of God.**
(Romans 3:23, NKJV)*

A

All have sinned, and this we know
that our Lord above still loves us so.
All we need is to come forth and say,
"Forgive me, Lord" when we pray!

A is for angel. Archangels acted as announcers!

Believe in the Lord Jesus, and you will be saved.
(Acts 16:31, NIV)

Believe in Jesus and be saved;
this will guide you on the way.
The path to Heaven is not wide,
but Christ is walking by your side.

B is for bee. Bees believe in blending better honey butter.

C

Choose for yourselves this day whom you will serve.
(Joshua 24:15b, NKJV)

Follow the leader is a fun game,
but following just anyone is not the same.
To serve two masters just won't do!
Make Jesus Christ the one for you.

C is for cat. Cuddling cute cats can cure your cantankerousness.

*Do not be afraid;
do not be discouraged.*
(Deuteronomy 31:8b, NIV)

Scary things go bump in the night; spooky sounds and shadows cause such a fright.
God says, "Don't be discouraged or afraid.
I will hold your hand and protect always."

D is for dragonfly. Darting dragonflies dive decidedly at ducks and dogs.

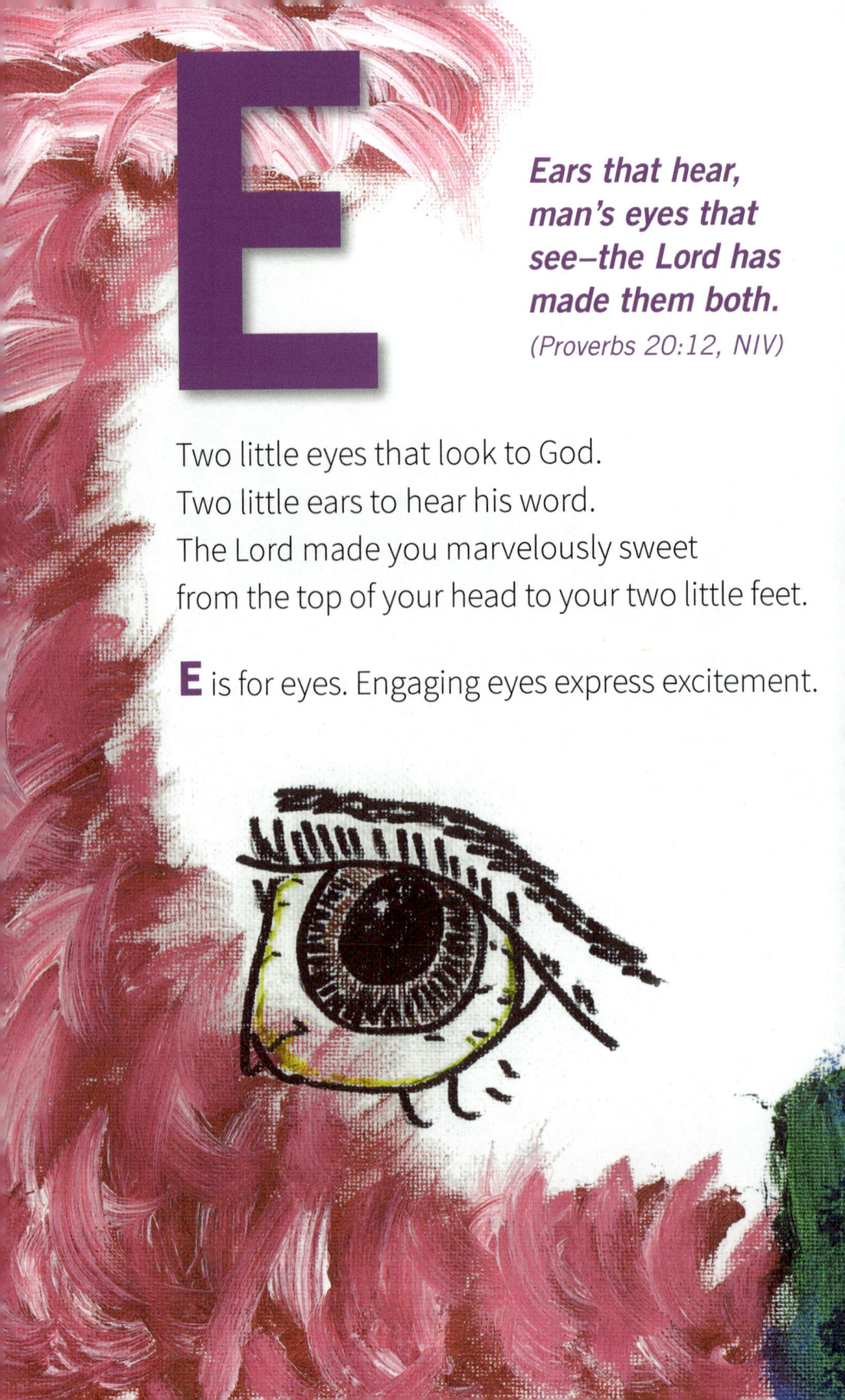

E

Ears that hear, man's eyes that see—the Lord has made them both.
(Proverbs 20:12, NIV)

Two little eyes that look to God.
Two little ears to hear his word.
The Lord made you marvelously sweet
from the top of your head to your two little feet.

E is for eyes. Engaging eyes express excitement.

Forgive as the Lord forgave you.
(Colossians 3:13, NIV)

To forgive and forget is easy to say;
it's not always easy to do.
But our Lord above calls us this very day
to forgive all others for the things they do.

F is for fish. Friendly fish flip and flop fearlessly.

Go and make disciples of all nations.
(Matthew 28:19, NIV)

Go out into the world around—
the word of God to spread.
The lost of the world to be found;
they need to know of our Living Head.

G is for goose. A giddy goose guffaws gloriously.

How great is the love the Father has lavished on us, that we should be called children of God!
(1 John 3:1, NIV)

Hear today of the great love of our Lord—
His blessed children we are.
He sacrificed himself to assure our reward.
His grace and mercy stretching afar.

H is for horse. Happy horses have healthy hearts!

In my Father's house are many mansions.
(John 14:2, NKJV)

In God's house are many rooms.
Heaven stands waiting for those who believe.
Jesus has gone to prepare a place for you in God's holy place, to live eternally.

I is for ice. Incredible ice inches along iridescently.

Judge me, O Lord, according to my righteousness, and according to my integrity, O Most High.
(Psalm 7:8, NKJV)

J

When you see what others do,
don't judge them good or bad.
Instead, help them see that they too
can find joy and peace in the Lord's hand.

J is for jester. Jesters jump and juggle jubilantly.

Keep my commands and you will live; guard my teachings as the apple of your eye.
(Proverbs 7:2, NKJV)

K

God gives to us his perfect will.
His commands guide us each day.
We hear his voice when quiet and still.
So guard his teachings in every way.

K is for king. Kind kings cannot contend with crafty knights.

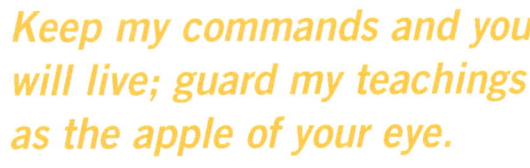

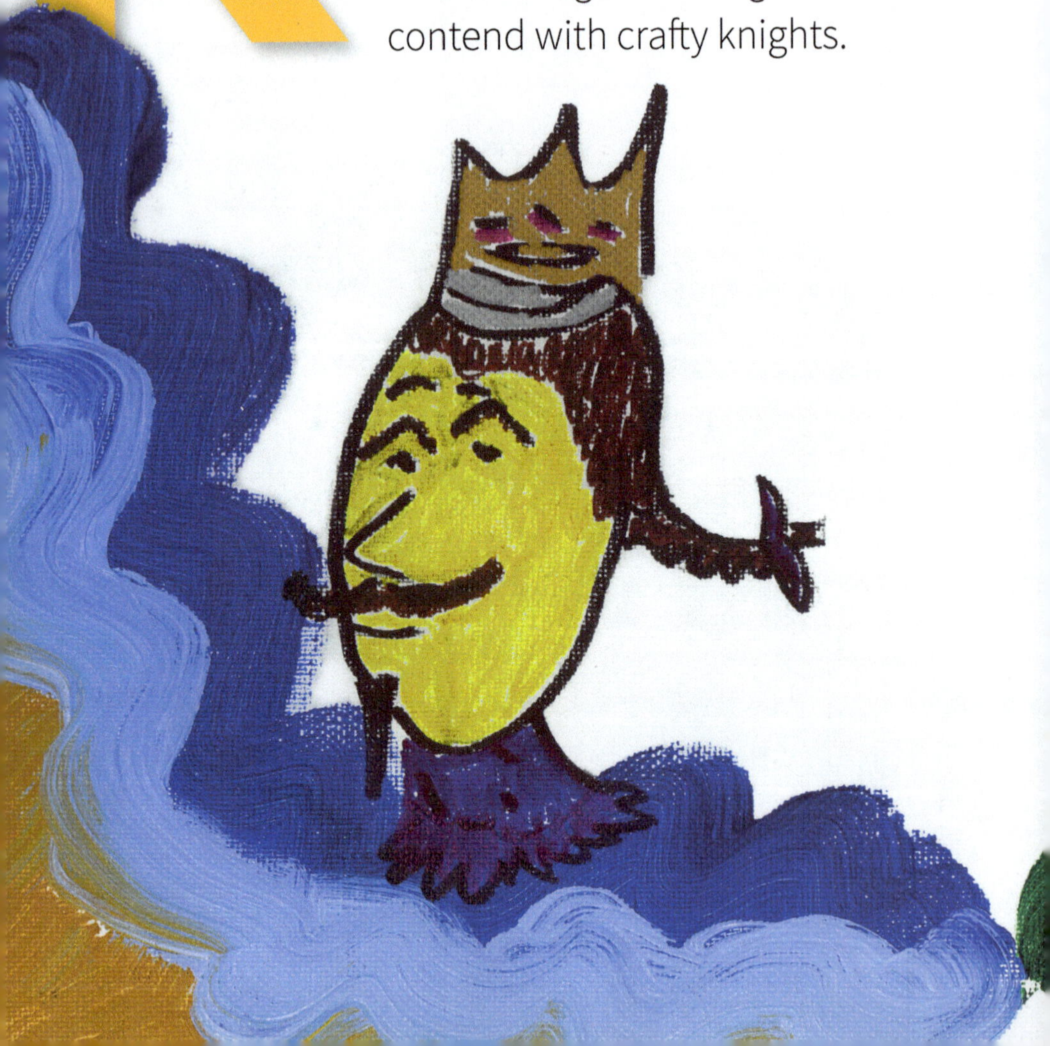

L

Love the Lord your God with all your heart and with all your soul and with all your strength.
(Deuteronomy 6:5, NIV)

Loving the Lord, what a joy divine!
All your body rejoices in His glory.
Raise up your hands and clap in time—
your heart, mind, and soul telling His story.

L is for lynx. Leaping lynxes land lightly.

Man shall not live on bread alone, but on every word that comes from the mouth of God.
(Matthew 4:4, NIV)

Breakfast, lunch, and dinner…Hey, it's time to eat!
But God is giving us a very special treat!
The wondrous word of God is being served today.
Take it! Eat it! Your life—it will save!

M is for monkey. Mischievous monkeys make many mistakes.

No one can redeem the life of another or give to God a ransom for them.
(Psalm 49:7, NIV)

Jesus our Lord paid a terrible price
to save us by giving up His life.
The precious gift was without compare,
since no one else the burden could share.

N is for nest. Nestled neatly in the nettles of a northern fir is a new nest.

Obey God rather than men.
(Acts 5:29b, NKJV)

Many people tell us what to do. Whom should we obey? When God gives instructions to you, you need to do what he says.

O is for oysters. Oysters only open on occasion.

*Praise be to the Lord, the God of Israel,
from everlasting to everlasting.*
(Psalm 41:13, NIV)

Sing praise to God always.
Sing praise to God always.
You are our King.
To everlasting,
sing praise to God always.

P is for puppies. Playful puppies perkily pounce in the pasture.

Q

Quietness and trust is your strength.
(Isaiah 30:15, NIV)

Silence is golden,
many would say;
to be still and quiet
Is a better way.
Through calm reflection,
we can find peace.
We build up our strength
in prayer that won't cease.

Q is for queen. Quizzically the queen called for quince.

Repent for the kingdom of heaven is at hand.
(Matthew 3:2, NKJV)

Repent is a fancy word that means "please forgive." We need to repent of our sin so that a life like Christ we live.

R is for rabbit. Rascally rabbits routinely ravage the rutabagas.

S

Seek first His kingdom and his righteousness.
(Matthew 6:33, NIV)

We go running after worldly things;
we think they'll make us glad.
But God wants us to seek him first,
and avoid those things that are bad.

S is for squirrel. Skittish squirrels scamper soundlessly.

Train up a child in the way he should go, and when he is old he will not depart from it.
(Proverbs 22:6, NKJV)

Growing up with God—what a precious gift!
Your life is a puzzle where all the pieces fit.
As you grow, you will learn the important wrongs and rights.
You will be prepared to face the difficult fights in life.

T is for turtle. Tiny turtles trundle tiredly toward the turning tide.

Upright One, you make the way of the righteous smooth.
(Isaiah 26:7, NKJV)

God watches over our paths through life.
This doesn't mean there won't be pain or strife.
But know that our Lord won't leave you in despair.
Run into His presence,
His protection to share.

U is for umbrella. Under umbrellas are unusual urchins.

*Vindicate me, my God...
rescue me from those who
are deceitful and wicked.*
(Psalm 43:1, NIV)

Sometimes we get mad and want to get even.
However, the Lord says "No!" to "even-Steven."
Instead, we need to pray for the guidance of
God's will.
Only He should punish those who do us ill.

V is for violin. Vigorous violin vendors vibrantly vent their views.

W

Walk in the way of righteousness, along the paths of justice.
(Proverbs 8:20, NIV)

As we go along life's narrow way,
Seeking the path of righteousness,
remember to walk with Jesus always.
For to follow Him is the path of justice.

W is for walrus. Wondering walruses waddle when wandering.

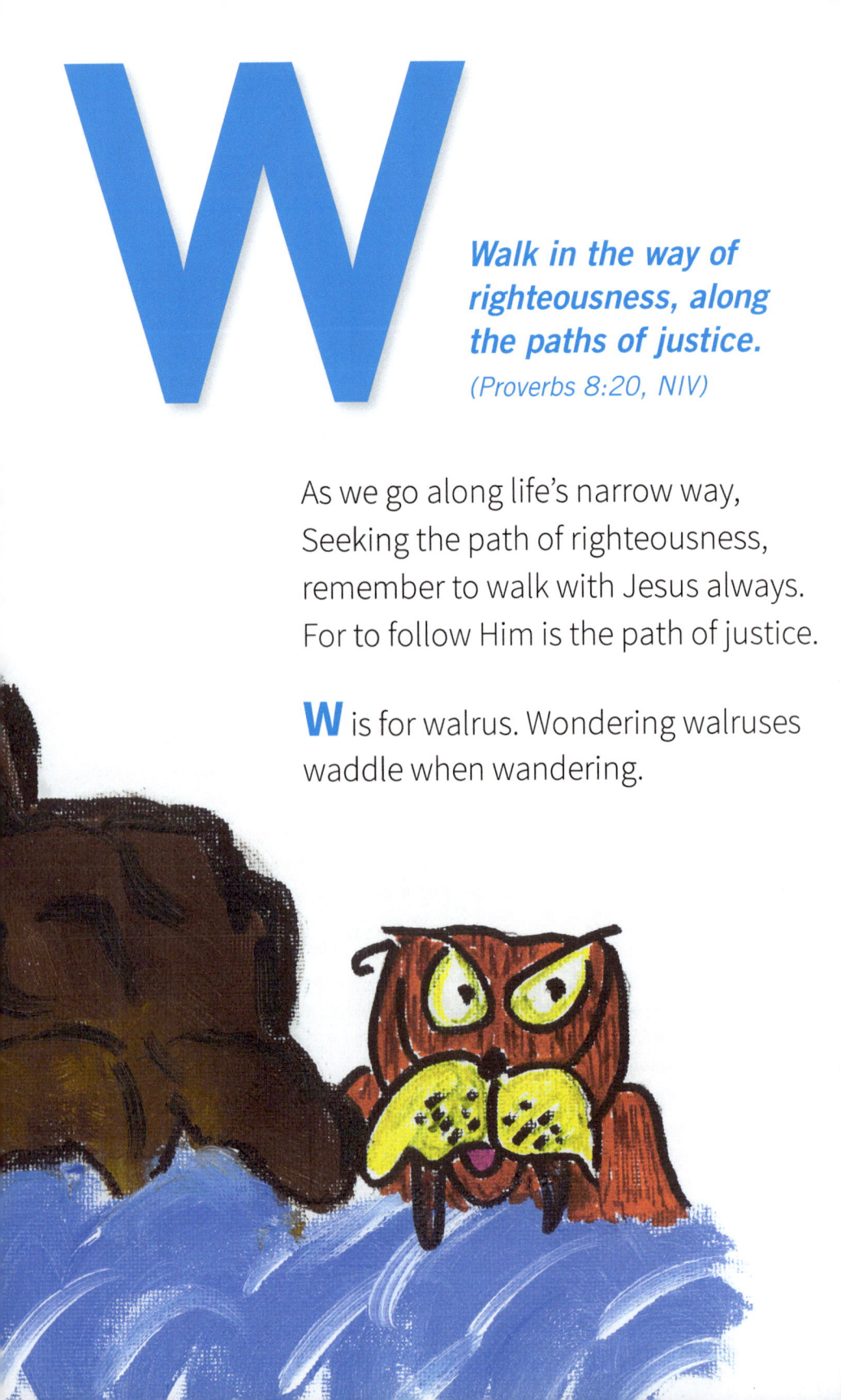

Xerxes, the king, asked, "What is it Queen Esther? What is your request? Even up to half the kingdom, it will be given to you."
(Esther 5:3, NIV)

King Xerxes' offer was grand indeed! Queen Esther could have asked for the moon!
We, too, as Christians need to petition God, for he stands waiting to hear our boon.

X is for xylophone. The xylophones exhibit extraordinary expertise.

You are the salt of the earth.
(Matthew 5:13a, NIV)

You are the salt of the earth.
What you do can make it or break it.
So, spread God's word, His love, His mirth.
You're salt of the earth, so SHAKE IT!

Y is for yak. Yaks usually find yellow yuccas yummy.

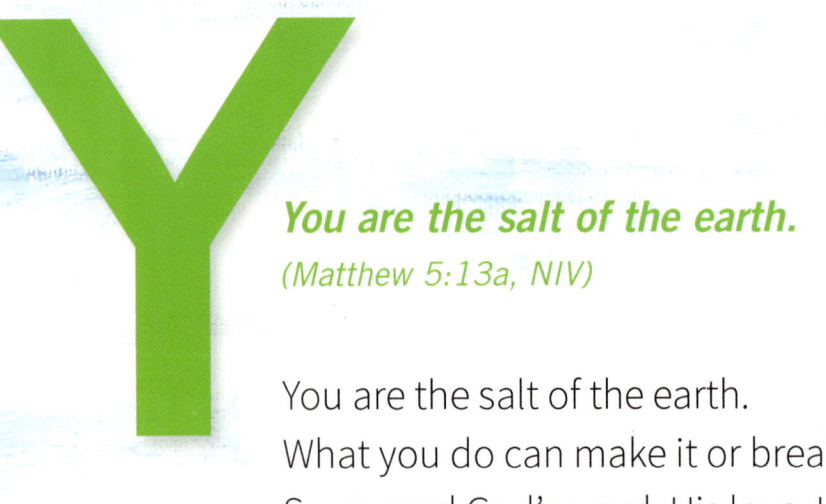

Zeal for your house (God) will consume me.
(John 2:17, NIV)

Oh Lord, to come and worship you,
is all that I desire!
Lord, lift my voice to heavenly heights
as a part of your holy choir!

Z is for zebra. Zippy zebras zealously zigzag.

www.ingramcontent.com/pod-product-compliance
Lightning Source LLC
Chambersburg PA
CBHW040310080426
42450CB00004BC/156